Fish

I am a little fish,
I see you and you see me,
Splash of colour in the sea.

Alexandria Turner, aged 8

For Jamie and Jeff, Alex, Ashley and Dulcie, with love — N. S. S.
For Peg — J. S.

Barefoot Books
124 Walcot Street
Bath
BA1 5BG

First published in Great Britain in 2002 by Barefoot Books Ltd

This book was typeset in Della Robbia, Goudy Handtooled
and Garamond Italic
The illustrations were prepared in coloured ink, watercolour, gouache and
pencil crayon on 300gsm watercolour paper

Graphic design by Applecart, Oxford
Colour separation by Grafiscan, Verona
Printed and bound in Singapore by Tien Wah Press (Pte) Ltd

This book has been printed on 100% acid-free paper

ISBN 1 84148 904 2

British Cataloguing-in-Publication Data: a catalogue record for this book is
available from the British Library

1 3 5 7 9 8 6 4 2

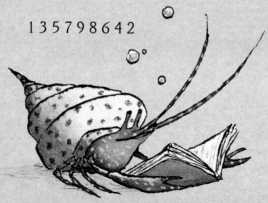

Sea Dream

Poems from under the Waves

compiled by **Nikki Siegen-Smith**

illustrated by **Joel Stewart**

Barefoot Books
Celebrating Art and Story

Contents

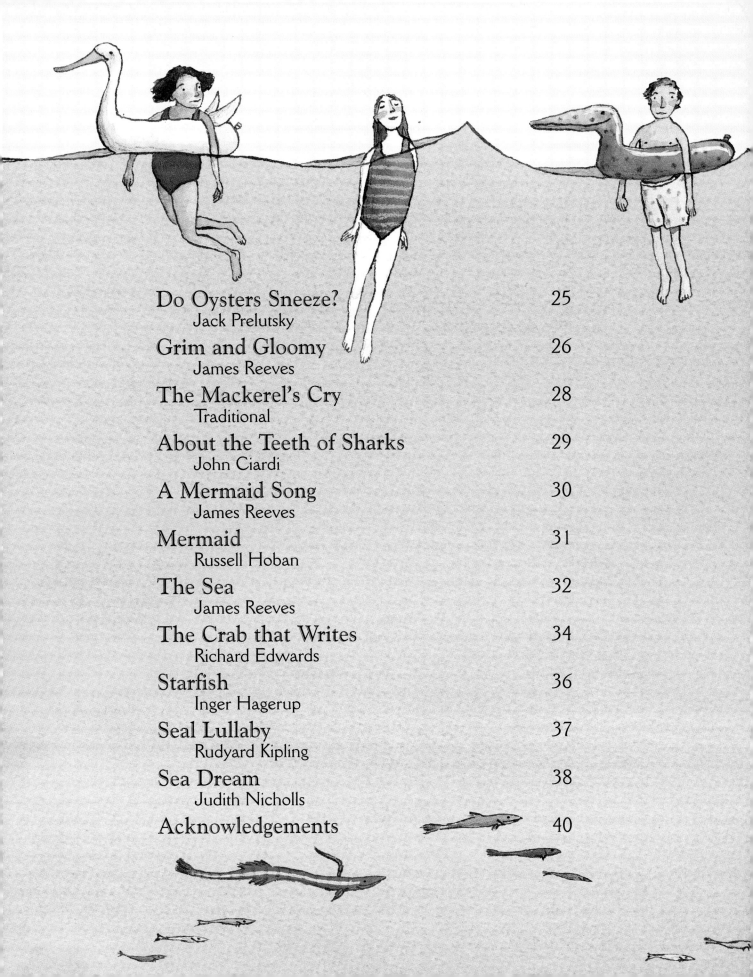

INTRODUCTION

Snorkelling with my masked eyes peering towards the seabed, salt water lapping in my ears, I see a jellyfish glide towards me, its milk-white tentacles trailing beneath. I want to stay and stare, but I also want to swim away fast, back to the beach. Above the water are sun, salt wind and sandy shore – the familiar. Under the water are bladderwrack and limpets, eels and whales – a mysterious world we rarely enter.

The poets in this collection take us over the beach – where the crab 'writes on the shining shore' – and down under the waves. With them we can plunge into the underwater world they conjure up for us and see sights that are sometimes scary – like J. F. Hendry's catfish, with its 'leopard eye of a murderer' and 'grip like steel'. We can view sea creatures in quirky ways: find out how Ozzie Octopus cheers himself up or learn how, from a sardine's viewpoint, a submarine is just a 'tin full of people'. And we can ponder such matters as whether oysters sneeze or starfish prefer to hang in the sky.

Some of the poems show us worlds within worlds. Walter de la Mare captures the 'pool in the rock' with its anemones, scallops and 'prowling mackerel' – a sea in miniature. For the batch of barnacles in Sam McBratney's poem, the only world they know is their patch of whale skin they cling to. They sail the seas on the tail of a whale and don't even know 'that they'd been away'.

In many of the poems, fact blurs into fantasy. I used never to be sure whether seahorses were real until I saw some swimming in an aquarium, with their little horse faces and curled tails. Even now they seem to hover somewhere between reality and make-believe. In Blake Morrison's poem 'Seahorse' we feel the rhythm of the tiny creatures galloping 'the seaweed lanes'. We go one step further into fantasy with Russell Hoban's 'Mermaid', 'green-glimmering in the deeps', and Judith Nicholls takes us into her evocative 'Sea Dream':

> *I wake to coral blossom*
> *and sleep in a star-clad cave;*
> *my bed is a glade*
> *of ribboned jade,*
> *my sky a wave.*

I hope you'll enjoy reading these poems to yourself and to others, in school, at home or in your hideout. Maybe you'll be inspired, like Alex Turner, to write a poem of your own, or illustrate your favourite one using Joel Stewart's wonderful illustrations as a starting point.

Nikki Siegen-Smith

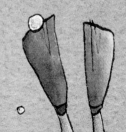

The Sea's Treasures

In swept the sea
With a swirl and a swish,
It shimmered and whispered,
'Choose what you wish.'

And the sea showed its treasures
At the edge of the shore,
Shining bright pebbles
And shells by the score.

Long ribbons of seaweed
That shone gold and red,
'I'll share them, I'll share,'
The sea softly said.

Daphne Lister

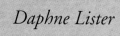
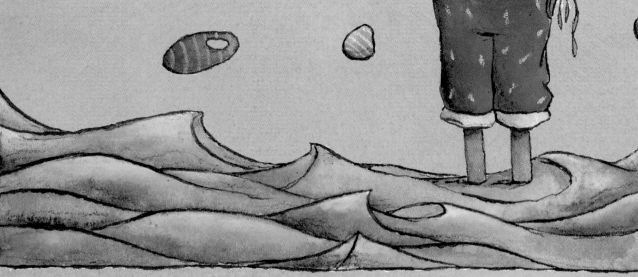

Fish

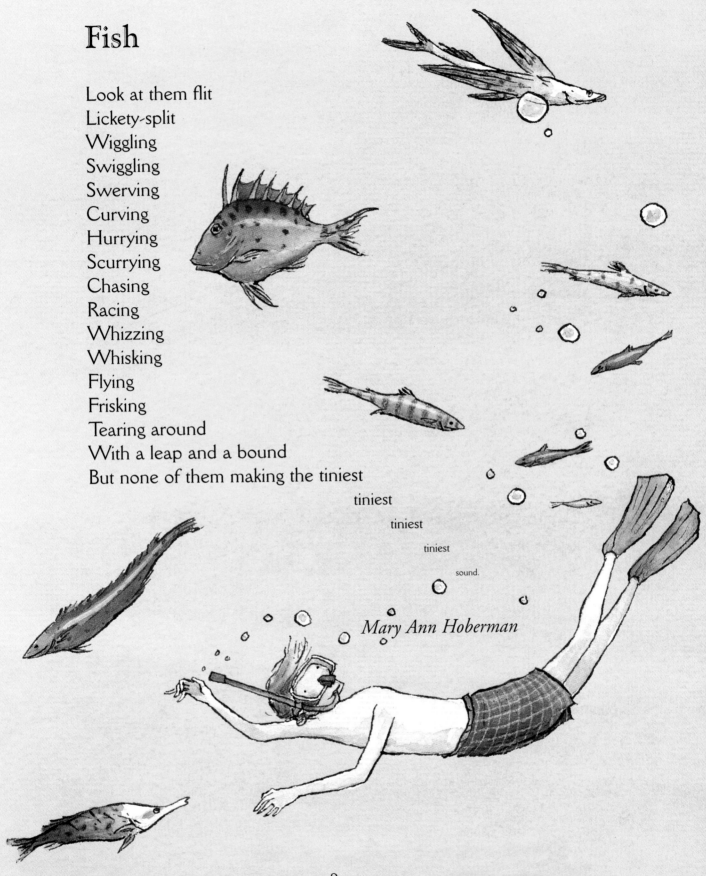

Look at them flit
Lickety-split
Wiggling
Swiggling
Swerving
Curving
Hurrying
Scurrying
Chasing
Racing
Whizzing
Whisking
Flying
Frisking
Tearing around
With a leap and a bound
But none of them making the tiniest
                  tiniest
                     tiniest
                        tiniest
                          sound.

Mary Ann Hoberman

Seal

See how he dives
From rocks with a zoom!
See how he darts
Through his watery room
Past crabs and eels
And green seaweed,
Past fluffs of sandy
Minnow feed!
See how he swims
With a swerve and a twist,
A flip of the flipper,
A flick of the wrist!
Quicksilver-quick,
Softer than spray,
Down he plunges
And sweeps away;
Before you can think,
Before you can utter
Words like 'Dill pickle'
Or 'Apple butter',
Back up he swims
Past sting-ray and shark,
Out with a zoom,
A whoop, a bark;
Before you can say
Whatever you wish,
He plops at your side
With a mouthful of fish!

William Jay Smith

Seahorse

O under the ocean waves
I gallop the seaweed lanes,
I jump the coral reef,
And all with no saddle or reins.

I haven't a flowing mane,
I've only this horsey face,
But under the ocean waves
I'm the king of the steeplechase.

Blake Morrison

Crab

In the low tide pools
I pack myself like
A handy pocket
Chest of tools.

But as the tide fills
Dancing I go
Under lifted veils
Tiptoe, tiptoe.

And with pliers and pincers
Repair and remake
The daintier dancers
The breakers break.

Ted Hughes

13

Phinniphin

The tide is in,
   The tide is in,
      The Phinniphin
         Are out.

They love the sea,
   The salty sea,
      Of this there is
         No doubt.

O watch them flop
   And slip and slop
      With clumsy hop
         Right past

The sandy beach
   Until they reach
      The friendly sea
         At last.

But when the tide,
   The shifty tide
      Stays right outside
         The bar,

They can't go in
   The Phinniphin:
      The Phinniphin
         Cannot go in:
            They'd have to hop
               Too far.

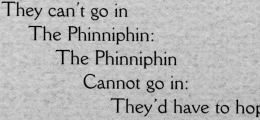

Frank Collymore

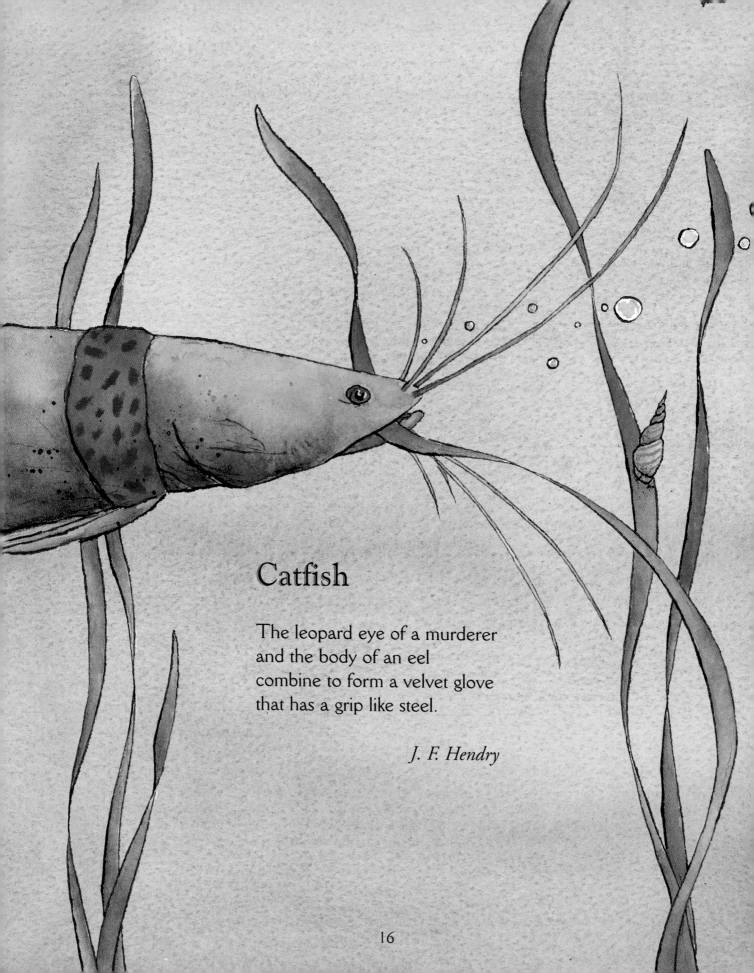

Catfish

The leopard eye of a murderer
and the body of an eel
combine to form a velvet glove
that has a grip like steel.

J. F. Hendry

O'er Seas That Have
No Beaches

O'er seas that have no beaches
To end their waves upon,
I floated with twelve peaches,
A sofa and a swan.

The blunt waves crashed above us
The sharp waves burst around,
There was no one to love us,
No hope of being found —

Where, on the notched horizon
So endlessly a-drip,
I saw all of a sudden
No sign of any ship.

Mervyn Peake

Ozzie Octopus

When Ozzie Octopus is sad —
An easy thing to be
When you are cold and lonely
At the bottom of the sea —
When Ozzie Octopus is glum
And far away from friends,
He stretches out his wavy legs
And curls them at the ends,
And soon starts laughing happily
And shaking just like jelly,
With all his eight legs tickling
His octopussy belly.

Richard Edwards

The Pool in the Rock

In this water, clear as air,
Lurks a lobster in its lair.
Rock-bound weed sways out and in,
Coral-red, and bottle green.
Wondrous pale anemones
Stir like flowers in a breeze:
Fluted scallop, whelk in shell,
And the prowling mackerel.
Winged with snow the sea-mews ride
The brine-keen wind; and far and wide
Sounds on the hollow thunder of the tide.

Walter de la Mare

The Whale

A whale!
  Down it goes, and more and more,
    up goes its tail!

Buson
Translated from the Japanese by H. G. Henderson

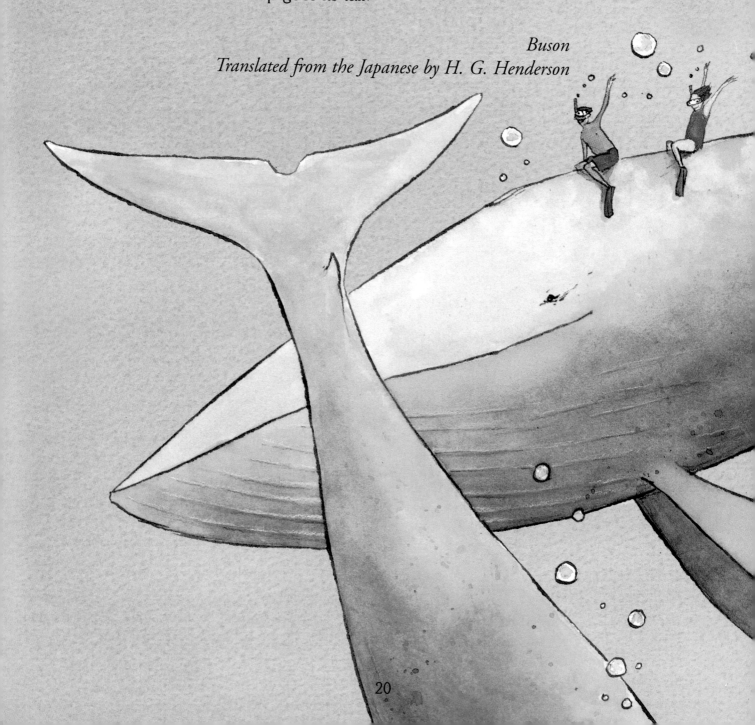

The Barnacle Batch

A batch of barnacles sailed the world
　on the back of a blue-nosed whale.
They were well stuck on with
　barnacle glue
　　to a spot near the end of the tail.

Now the whale didn't know
that they were there,
so she didn't ask them
to pay a fare.
And the barnacle batch
didn't offer to pay,
for they weren't aware
that they'd been away.

Sam McBratney

A Baby Sardine

A baby sardine
Saw her first submarine:
She was scared and watched through
  a peephole.
'Oh, come, come, come,'
Said the sardine's mum,
'It's only a tin full of people.'

Spike Milligan

The Little Turtle

There was a little turtle.
He lived in a box.
He swam in a puddle.
He climbed on the rocks.

He snapped at a mosquito.
He snapped at a flea.
He snapped at a minnow.
And he snapped at me.

He caught the mosquito.
He caught the flea.
He caught the minnow.
But he didn't catch me.

Vachel Lindsay

The Jellyfish

The jellyfish,
Is not a smelly fish,
That much is quite apparent.
They don't have things
Like scales or fins,
In actual fact,
They're transparent.

Yet whenever fish have parties
As birthday treats
For their fry.
They always invite the jellyfish
And I can't think of one reason why.

Richard Digance

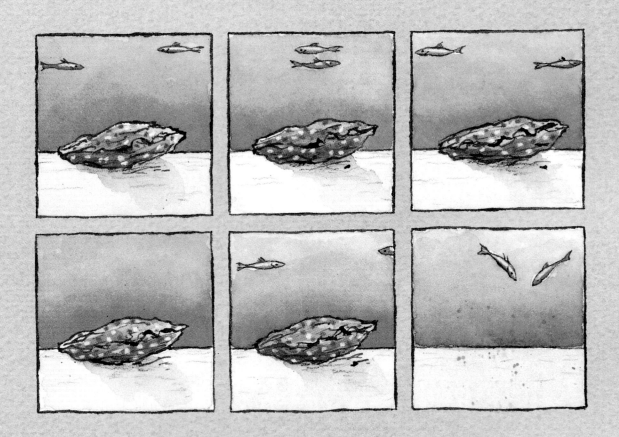

Do Oysters Sneeze?

Do oysters sneeze beneath the seas,
or wiggle to and fro,
or sulk, or smile, or dance awhile
…how can we ever know?

Do oysters yawn when roused at dawn,
and do they ever weep,
and can we tell, when, in its shell,
an oyster is asleep?

Jack Prelutsky

Grim and Gloomy

Oh, grim and gloomy,
So grim and gloomy
Are the caves beneath the sea.
Oh, rare but roomy
And bare and boomy,
Those salt sea caverns be.

Oh, slim and slimy
Or grey and grimy
Are the animals of the sea.
Salt and oozy
And safe and snoozy
The caves where those animals be.

Hark to the shuffling,
Huge and snuffling,
Ravenous, cavernous, great sea-beasts!
But fair and fabulous,
Tintinnabulous,
Gay and fabulous are their feasts.

Ah, but the queen of the sea,
The querulous, perilous sea!
How the curls of her tresses
The pearls on her dresses,
Sway and swirl in the waves,
How cosy and dozy,
How sweet ring-a-rosy
Her bower in the deep-sea caves!

Oh, rare but roomy
And bare and boomy
Those caverns under the sea,
And grave and grandiose
Safe and sandiose
The dens of her denizens be.

James Reeves

The mackerel's cry
Is never long dry.

Traditional

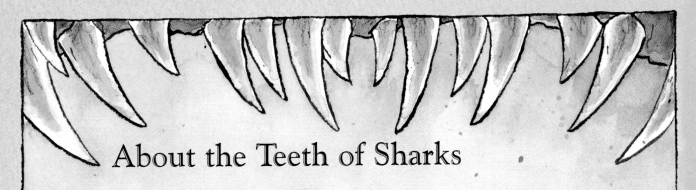

About the Teeth of Sharks

The thing about a shark is — teeth,
One row above, one row beneath.

Now take a close look. Do you find
It has another row behind?

Still closer — here, I'll hold your hat:
Has it a third row behind that?

Now look in and…Look out! Oh my,
I'll *never* know now! Well, goodbye.

John Ciardi

A Mermaid Song

She sits by the sea in the clear, shining air,
   And the sailors call her Moonlight, Moonlight;
They see her smoothing her wavy hair
   And they hear her singing, singing.
The sea-shells learn their tunes from her
And the big fish listen with never a stir
   To catch the voice of Moonlight, Moonlight,
And I would hark for a year and a year
   To hear her singing, singing.

James Reeves

Mermaid

Mermaid, mermaid,
green-glimmering in the deeps,
pearly-naked gliding
where the Kraken sleeps!
Ancient is the ocean of my mind;
in its full-moon waters
you I find,
mermaid!

Russell Hoban

The Sea

The sea is a hungry dog,
Giant and grey.
He rolls on the beach all day.
With his clashing teeth and shaggy jaws
Hour upon hour he gnaws
The rumbling, tumbling stones,
And 'Bones, bones, bones, bones!'
The giant sea-dog moans,
Licking his greasy paws.

And when the night wind roars
And the moon rocks in the stormy cloud,
He bounds to his feet and snuffs and sniffs,
Shaking his wet sides all over the cliffs,
And howls and hollos long and loud.

But on quiet days in May or June,
When even the grasses on the dune
Play no more their reedy tune,
With his head between his paws
He lies on the sandy shores,
So quiet, so quiet, he scarcely snores.

James Reeves

The Crab that Writes

When the tide is low on moonlit nights,
Out of the sea crawls the crab that writes,
Out of the sea crawls the crab whose claw
Writes these words on the shining shore:

PEBBLE MUSSEL
FIN AND SCALE
SOLE AND MACKEREL
SKATE AND WHALE
SEAWEED STARFISH
SALT AND STONE
SAND AND SHELL AND CUTTLEBONE.

When the tide is low on moonlit nights,
Back to the sea crawls the crab that writes,
Back to the sea crawls the crab whose claw
Leaves these words on the shining shore:

PEBBLE MUSSEL
FIN AND SCALE
SOLE AND MACKEREL
SKATE AND WHALE
SEAWEED STARFISH
SALT AND STONE
SAND AND SHELL AND CUTTLEBONE.

Richard Edwards

Starfish

The stars blink bright up there on high
hidden behind the dark blue sky.
The starfish lies on the ocean bed
no hands, nor feet, nor legs, nor head.
It likes it there
and would not care
to hang in the midnight sky.

Inger Hagerup
Translated by Joan Tate

Seal Lullaby

Oh! hush thee, my baby, the night is behind us,
And black are the waters that sparkled so green.
The moon, o'er the combers, looks downward to find us
At rest in the hollows that rustle between.

Where billow meets billow, there soft be thy pillow:
Ah, weary wee flipperling, curl at thy ease!
The storm shall not wake thee, nor shark overtake thee,
Asleep in the arms of the slow-swinging seas.

Rudyard Kipling

Sea Dream

I wander the deep-sea forests
where the snake-fish slither;
where the dark dunes drift
like rolling mist
and the white whales murmur.

I wake to coral blossom
and sleep in a star-clad cave;
my bed is a glade
of ribboned jade,
my sky a wave.

I dance by the spiny urchin
and ride the giant clam;
I feel as I sail
the dolphin's tail
the sad whale song.

Judith Nicholls

ACKNOWLEDGEMENTS

'The Whale' by Buson from *An Introduction to Haiku* by Harold G. Henderson, copyright © 1958 by Harold G. Henderson, used with permission of Doubleday, a division of Random House, Inc. 'About the Teeth of Sharks' by John Ciardi from *The New Oxford Treasury of Children's Poems*, copyright © John Ciardi, published by Oxford University Press. 'Phinniphin' by Frank Collymore from *A Caribbean Dozen*, compiled by John Agard and Grace Nichols, copyright © the Frank Collymore Estate, published by Walker Books Ltd 1994. 'The Jellyfish' by Richard Digance from *Another Animal Alphabet*, copyright © 1982 Richard Digance, published by Michael Joseph 1982. 'Starfish' by Inger Hagerup, original Norwegian poem copyright © Inger Hagerup, translated by Joan Tate, translation copyright © Joan Tate, published in Great Britain by Pelham Books Ltd 1979. 'Catfish' by J.F. Hendry from *A Scottish Poetry*, copyright © J. F. Hendry, published by Oxford University Press 1985. 'Mermaid' by Russell Hoban, copyright © 1997 Russell Hoban, from *The Last of the Wallendas and Other Poems*, published by Hodder and Stoughton. 'Fish' by Mary Ann Hoberman from *Hello and Goodbye*, copyright © 1959, renewed 1987 by Mary Ann Hoberman, published by Little, Brown and Co. 'Crab' from *The Mermaid's Purse* by Ted Hughes, copyright © 1999 by The Estate of Ted Hughes, used in the US by permission of Alfred A. Knopf Children's Books, a division of Random House, Inc.; used in the UK by permission of Faber and Faber Ltd. 'Seal Lullaby' by Rudyard Kipling from *Poems About Animals*, reprinted with permission of A. P. Watt Ltd on behalf of The National Trust for Places of Historical Interest or Natural Beauty. 'The Little Turtle' by Vachel Lindsay from *Collected Poems of Vachel Lindsay*, copyright © renewed 1948 by Elizabeth Lindsay, published by Macmillan Publishers Ltd 1920. 'The Sea's Treasures' by Daphne Lister from *Sit on the Roof and Holler*, collected by Adrian Rumble, published by Bell & Hyman 1984, copyright © Daphne Lister 1984. 'The Pool in the Rock' by Walter de la Mare, reprinted with permission from the Literary Trustees of Walter de la Mare and the Society of Authors as their representative. 'The Barnacle Batch' by Sam McBratney from *Long, Tall, Short and Hairy Poems*, copyright © 1996 Sam McBratney, reproduced by permission of Hodder and Stoughton Limited. 'A Baby Sardine' from *A Book of Milliganimals* by Spike Milligan, used with permission of Spike Milligan Productions Ltd. 'Seahorse' by Blake Morrison, copyright © 1991 Blake Morrison. 'Sea Dream' from *Midnight Forest* by Judith Nicholls, copyright © 1985 Judith Nicholls, published by Faber and Faber Ltd. 'O'er Seas That Have No Beaches' by Mervyn Peake from *The Puffin Book of Nonsense Verse*, copyright © The Estate of Mervyn Peake, published by The Penguin Group 1996. 'Do Oysters Sneeze?' from *The New Kid On The Block* by Jack Prelutsky, copyright © 1984 Jack Prelutsky, published in the UK by Heinemann Young Books, an imprint of Egmont Books Ltd, London, and in the US by HarperCollins Publishers; used with permission. 'Grim and Gloomy', 'Mermaid Song' and 'The Sea' by James Reeves from *Complete Poems for Children*, copyright © James Reeves, published by Heinemann. Reprinted by permission of the James Reeves Estate. 'Seal' by William Jay Smith from *Laughing Time: Collected Nonsense*, copyright © 1990 by William Jay Smith, reprinted with permission of Farrar, Straus and Giroux, LLC. 'Ozzie Octopus' and 'The Crab that Writes' by Richard Edwards from *Moon Frog*, copyright © 1992 Richard Edwards, illustrations copyright © 1992 Sarah Fox Davies. Reproduced by permission of the publisher, Walker Books Ltd., London.

Special thanks to Alexandria Turner for 'Fish', copyright © Alexandria Turner.

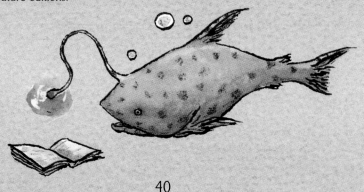

Barefoot Books
Celebrating Art and Story

At Barefoot Books, we celebrate art and story with books that open the hearts and minds of children from all walks of life, inspiring them to read deeper, search further, and explore their own creative gifts. Taking our inspiration from many different cultures, we focus on themes that encourage independence of spirit, enthusiasm for learning, and acceptance of other traditions. Thoughtfully prepared by writers, artists and storytellers from all over the world, our products combine the best of the present with the best of the past to educate our children as the caretakers of tomorrow. *www.barefootbooks.com*

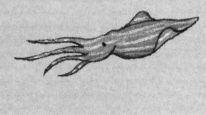

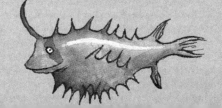